Probate and Estate Administration

View Legal

WORKBOOK

MATTHEW BURGESS

National Library of Australia Cataloguing-in-Publication entry

Creator: Burgess, Matthew, 1973- author.

Title: Probate and Estate Administration / Matthew Burgess; book designed by Dedicated Book Services.

ISBN: 978-1-925406-99-3 (paperback)

Subjects: Burgess, Matthew.
View Legal (Firm)
Legal services—Australia.
Finance, Personal—Australia.
Assets (Accounting)—Australia.
Tax planning—Australia.
Estate planning—Australia.

Other Creators/Contributors: Dedicated Book Services, book designer.

Probate and Estate Administration—Workbook

Published by D & M Fancy Pastry in 2018

Typefaces: ElectraLTStd

Contents

Introduction

Matthew Burgess, Patrick Ellwood and Tara Lucke are co founders, with Naomi Arnold, of View Legal.

Having previously founded Australia's first virtual law firm as a wholly owned subsidiary of one of the country's leading independent law firms, View Legal is results focused and passionate about delivering new solutions in a way that aligns with their 'SPS'—service and price satisfaction guarantee.

As author of technical legal books, Matthew is widely recognised as constantly creating innovative strategies for the growth, management and protection of wealth.

Published legal books include:

(1) The Nine Steps to a Complete Estate Plan
(2) The Seven Foundations of Business Succession
(3) Five Essential Estate Planning Articles
(4) The Seven Key Aspects of Testamentary Trusts
(5) Inside Stories—the complete collection of blog posts
(6) The Five Foundations of SMSFs
(7) Six Foundations of the Taxation of Trusts
(8) Six Essential Structuring Articles
(9) The Nine Foundations of Asset Protection

Chapter 1

Overview

NOTES

OVERVIEW

There was significant commentary about the apparently overwhelming number of 'celebrity' deaths in 2016.

There are however many who believe that 2016 merely marked the start of the 'new normal' in relation to the death rates of well-known celebrities and indeed death rates generally.

Arguably the two primary reasons for this were:

(1) the baby boomer population bubble; and
(2) 'Big Bang Disruption' theory.

The socioeconomic impact of the baby boomer generation as it has moved through the lifecycle is well documented.

Even the youngest baby boomers are now in their 50s, and the oldest are into their 70s.

While the baby boomer generation has caused a 'bubble' at each other stage of their lifecycle, because of the way life expectancies are spread, it is likely that instead of a bubble, there will be instead a jump up in overall deaths that will be sustained over a long period. In other words, reinforcing the idea that 2016 was simply the start of the 'new normal' for deaths of popular culture icons and indeed death rates more generally.

This outcome is arguably further reinforced by the significant growth in elder suicide rates in recent times.

In the context of the above themes, estate planning is widely considered the 'new black' for many advisers.

The 'next wave' for advisers, particularly as the baby boomer generation enters the last phase of their life span, is probate and estate administration.

The administration of a deceased estate is a heavily regulated area and there are many aspects that can cause irreversible damage if misunderstood.

This Workbook explores the key issues that advisers need to know in relation to the administration of any deceased estate, including—

(1) Discussion about what probate is exactly, when is it needed and how do you get it
(2) Exploration of the key steps in obtaining probate
(3) Analysing the key steps in estate administration
(4) Identifying the key areas where advisers can add value
(5) Specific examples
(6) Key checklists

View's web-based estate planning platform is designed to be the solution of choice by leading advisers wanting to offer a facilitated or project managed outcome.

The platform also offers, nationwide, a comprehensive adviser centric solution for probate and estate administration.

This Workbook is ultimately designed to help financial advisers, accountants, risk advisers and other lawyers to radically expand their estate planning related offerings to be both 'front end' (i.e. wills, powers of attorney and memos of directions) and 'back end' (i.e. probate and estate administration).

GLOSSARY

A glossary of the key abbreviations used in this book is as follows:

- ATO—Australian Taxation Office;
- BDBN—binding death benefit nomination;
- CGT—capital gains tax;
- EPT—estate proceeds trust;
- FPA—family provision application;
- LPR—legal personal representative;
- MoD—memo of directions;
- NSW—New South Wales;
- SMSF—self-managed superannuation fund;
- SPT—superannuation proceeds trust;
- TFM—testator's family maintenance;
- TT—testamentary trust;
- UPE—unpaid present entitlement.

WORKBOOK FORMAT

The format of this book is as follows:

- Overview of each key concept generally;
- Diagram and bullet point explanation of each key concept;
- Assets and liabilities checklist;
- Estate administration checklist.

Chapter 2

The detail and diagrams

KEY MANTRAS

The leading mantras for estate planning are profiled in complementary View book 'Estate Planning War Stories' and are summarised on the next page.

3 THINGS

No estate plan = estate plan
Estate planning is more than just a will
Don't become a war story

ASSETS OUTSIDE OF ESTATE

Perhaps one of the most important aspects of modern estate planning is in relation to those assets which do not in fact pass pursuant to a person's will.

It is vital in any estate administration exercise, from as early as possible in the process, to clearly understand which assets are regulated by the person's will and which assets will need to be regulated utilising other strategies.

A brief summary of the main types of assets that do not pass pursuant to a person's will follows.

The table is not intended to be an exhaustive list of assets that fall outside a person's will. Rather it is provided to highlight the importance for clients to work with all their advisers including their financial planner, accountant, lawyer and insurance adviser in any estate administration exercise.

START AT THE START—UNDERSTAND ESTATE

① Estate assets

② Non-estate assets

③ Asset type

④ Control

⑤ Regulating documents

ASSETS WHICH DO NOT FORM PART OF ESTATE

(Part I)

Asset Type	Control	Documents Regulating
Joint tenancy (as opposed to tenants in common)	Survivor	Position at law
Superannuation (binding nomination)	Member within three years of death	Valid binding nomination
Superannuation (no binding nomination)	Fund trustee post death	Trust deed or terms of pension
Discretionary trust (individual trustee)	Appointor/principal, or in the absence of both, surviving trustee. If no surviving trustee, then legal personal representative of estate	Trust deed or trusts Act
Discretionary trustee (corporate trustee)	Appointor/principal, or in the absence of both, remaining directors of corporate trustee, subject to the shareholder's power to remove	Trust deed or constitution for corporate trustee

ASSETS WHICH DO NOT FORM PART OF ESTATE

(Part II)

Asset Type	Control	Documents Regulating
Unit trust	As above for discretionary trusts	Ultimate benefit in trust regulated by trust deed and unit holdings
Private company	Director subject to appointment by shareholders	Constitution or shareholders agreement. Transfer of shares may be pursuant to will depending on other documentation
Loan to company or trust	Lender or legal personal representative of lender	Loan agreement may override will
Business interests	Remaining business owners/ trustee of will	Business succession agreement/ partnership Act
Life insurance	Policy owner or nominated beneficiary	Insurance policy

PROBATE

When a person dies with a valid will, whoever is nominated as executor may apply to the court in the jurisdiction the deceased was domiciled to obtain a grant of probate (or a grant of 'administration') of the will.

Probate is confirmation from the court that the will of the deceased is the last valid will. Probate allows the executor to:

(1) collect the assets of the estate;
(2) pay the deceased's liabilities; and
(3) distribute the balance of the deceased's wealth in accordance with the terms of the will.

Probate is often required by third parties before assets of the deceased are released for distribution in accordance with the will.

SUMMARY OF KEY CONCEPTS

1. General overview of the estate administration process
2. Explanation of key roles in the estate administration process
3. Focus on grants and applications required
4. Have the confidence to expand the offering into this area
5. Analyse the advisers' role as a facilitator
6. Highlight key opportunities for advisers in this space

ESTATE ADMINISTRATION PROCESS

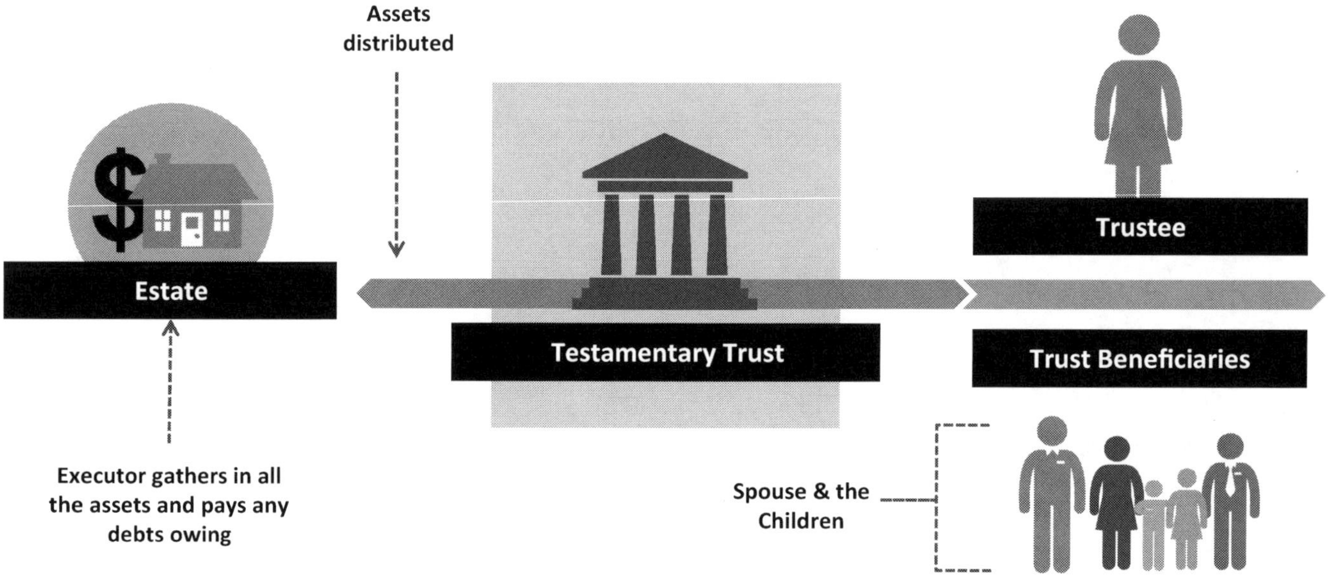

KEY ROLES

① Executor

② Administrator

③ Guardian (of infants)

④ Residue Beneficiary

⑤ Specific Beneficiary

⑥ Adviser

EXECUTOR

An executor has a number of duties and obligations in administering an estate.

The executor holds all of the assets of the deceased until they are distributed in accordance with the will.

The duties of an executor are many and include to:

(1) supervise the funeral arrangements;
(2) find the last will;
(3) obtain probate, if required;
(4) call in the assets of the estate: this often involves applying to the court for permission to deal with the assets under the will and collecting all assets and debts due to the estate;
(5) pay all outstanding debts: ideally this should be done within 12 months of the date of death, but the court can allow a longer period if it is reasonable in the circumstances;
(6) invest estate funds so as to earn interest whilst the estate is being administered;
(7) insure the assets of the estate against fire and other risks;
(8) distribute the assets in accordance with the will; and
(9) arrange the completion of tax returns for both the testator and the testator's estate.

It is important that at least one executor be appointed by the will. However, it is common that a back-up or alternative executor is appointed, in case one of the named executors is unable to act, or does not wish to act.

No more than four persons may apply to the court for permission to administer the estate.

If the executors cannot agree on the administration of the will, they will need to apply to the court for a ruling.

ROLE OF EXECUTOR/ADMINISTRATOR

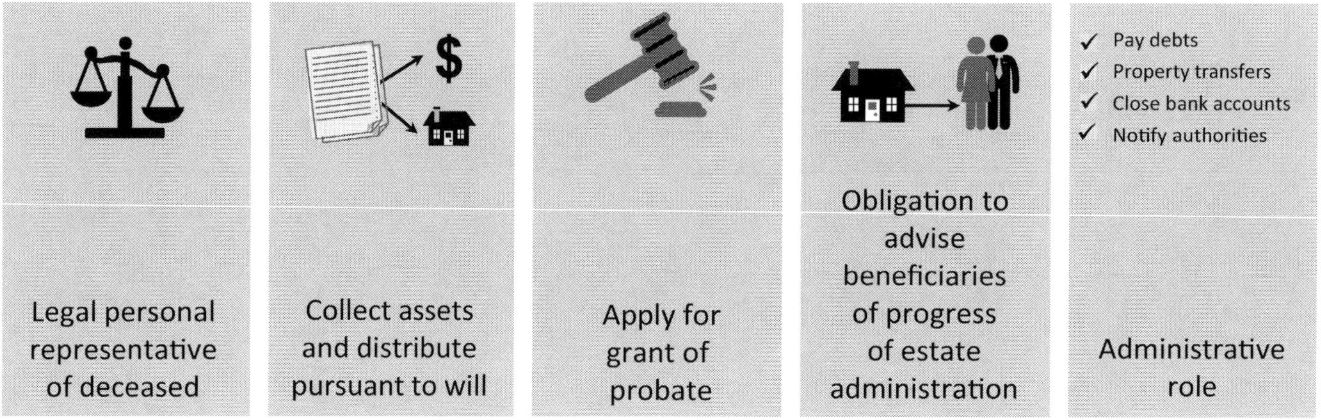

GUARDIANS (pastoral care of infant kids)

①	Legal guardian for minors
②	Nominated by the will
③	Will generally be the surviving biological parent (even if separated, subject to any contrary court orders)
④	Recommend multiple successive guardians be appointed

BENEFICIARIES

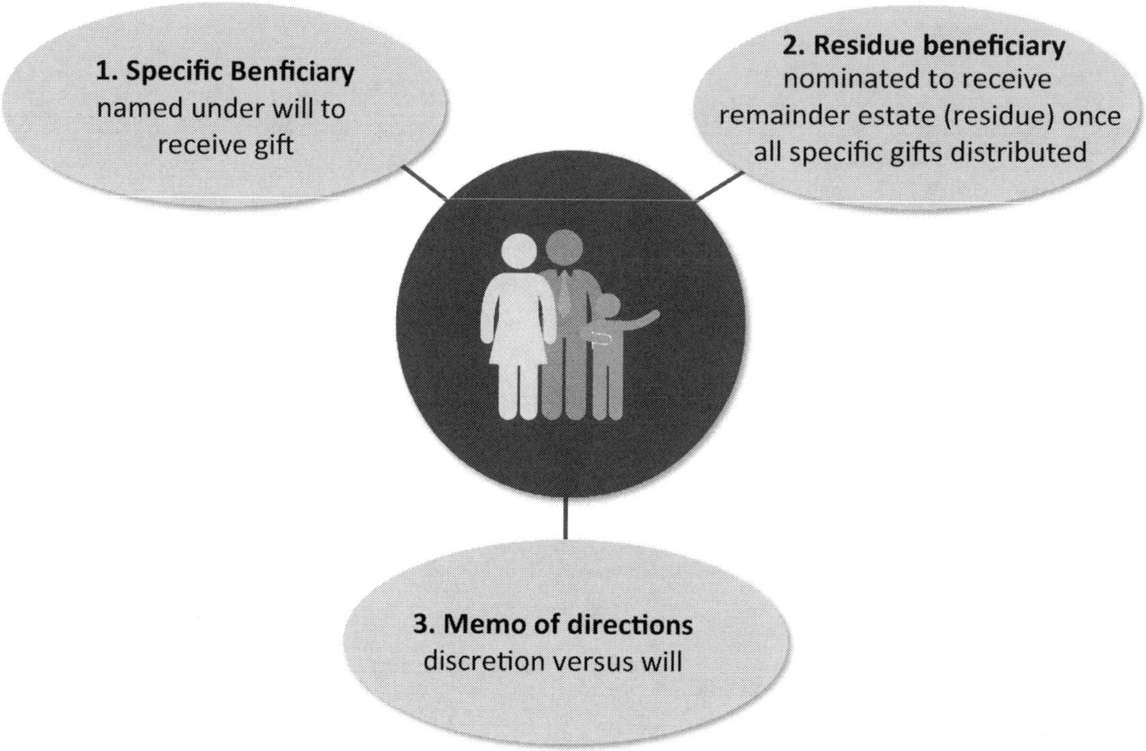

ADVISER'S ROLE

1. Preparation of an asset register of the estate
2. Location of and distribution of assets within the estate
3. Explain deceased and current investment strategy
4. Probate
5. Investment advice for beneficiaries

RESPONSIBILITIES

Once the executor has permission from the court to deal with the estate, they must act promptly to collect all the assets and debts of the estate.

They may be held personally liable for any loss suffered through their neglect.

If the executor fails to invest the assets of the estate, they may be liable to pay the interest that would have gone to the beneficiaries had the assets been properly invested.

If no executor is named in the will, it becomes necessary to apply to the court, so that the court can appoint someone to administer the deceased estate.

When appointing an administrator, the court will have regard to the rights of those people who are interested in the real and personal estate of the testator.

The court will appoint someone who has an interest in the residuary estate, but has the discretion to appoint someone else, if the circumstances warrant.

Generally, the court in its discretion can approve payment to an executor for their work in administration of the estate.

Applying to court for remuneration can be expensive and time consuming. An alternative approach is for all beneficiaries to agree the appropriate payment, provided all beneficiaries are adults who are not under a legal disability.

Assuming there are no complications with the deceased estate due to, for example, a challenge against a will, it is generally the case that the ATO accepts a maximum period of three years for an estate to be administered.

The administration of the estate, from the ATO's perspective involves the ultimate distribution of assets to beneficiaries if there is no formal testamentary trust under a will, or the distribution of assets to a testamentary trust if the deceased has incorporated that into their will.

It is important to note that while the ATO allows a maximum of three years, often they will in fact expect that the deceased estate is administered within 12 months from the date of death, and therefore may deny access to the excepted trust income provisions (these are the rules that allow children to be treated as adults for tax purposes) despite the fact that the executor may not believe the estate has been fully administered.

Pending formal advice from the accountant for the estate, the executor will be required to ensure they:

(1) prepare an individual tax return from 1 July in the tax year the deceased died until the date of death;
(2) obtain a tax file number for the estate and prepare a tax return for the period starting on the date of death until to 30 June in the tax year of death;
(3) prepare another tax return for the estate starting on 1 July in the next tax year following the date of death and ending when the estate is fully administered; and
(4) obtain tax file numbers for any testamentary trust and ensure that annual tax returns are prepared for the testamentary trust, once the estate is fully administered.

ESTATE ADMINISTRATION PROCESS

① Initial administration

② Communicate with beneficiaries

③ Collect cash assets and pay outstanding debts

④ Sell or transfer remaining assets

⑤ Determine superannuation entitlements

⑥ Make distributions according to will

⑦ Register death on joint tenancy assets

⑧ Taxation matters e.g. lodgement of tax return

DEALING WITH FINANCIAL INSTITUTIONS

1. Funeral costs
2. Debts
3. Credit cards
4. Direct Debits

PROBATE PROCESS

The executor of a deceased's will must advertise their intention to apply for probate in:

(1) a local newspaper (approved by the court) circulated in the place where the deceased resided immediately prior to their death; and
(2) various government bulletins.

The probate application can only be filed two weeks after the advertisement has last been published.

A 'tear sheet' proving the newspaper advertisement appeared needs to be lodged with the Public Trustee.

The probate application generally contains:

(1) a formal application; and
(2) a supporting affidavit by the executor.

The death certificate and a copy of the original will of the deceased must be attached to the supporting affidavit sworn by the executor.

The original will must also be provided to the court.

The court will normally issue a grant of administration within eight weeks from the date the application is filed.

The granting of probate is subject to the rights of anyone seeking to challenge the provisions of the will, often referred to as a 'family provision application'. The law in relation to family provision applications is complex and specialist advice should be obtained if this issue arises.

DEATH WITH A VALID WILL

Death certificate	Location of current valid will	Notice/ advertising of intended application	Application lodged	Grant of probate issued
		... for the grant of probate or letters of administration to be **published**	... with the courts for the grant of administration – **at least 14 days after the notice**	**5 days to 6 weeks from the date of application –** depends on the State / Territory and the complexity of the matter

GRANT

A formal recognition by the Court that the person applying has the authority to collect the assests of the deceased, pay the liabilities and distribute the balance

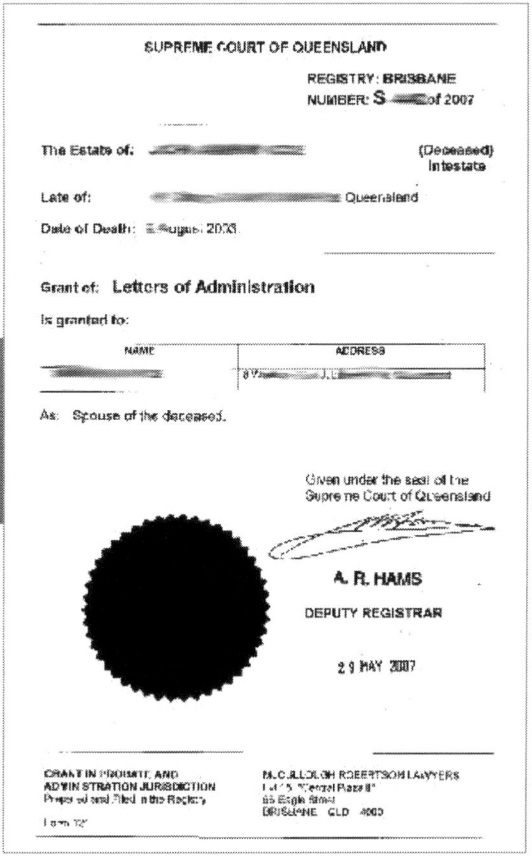

SUPREME COURT OF QUEENSLAND

REGISTRY: BRISBANE
NUMBER: S[redacted] of 2007

The Estate of: [redacted] (Deceased) Intestate

Late of: [redacted] Queensland

Date of Death: [redacted] August 2003

Grant of: **Letters of Administration**

Is granted to:

NAME	ADDRESS
[redacted]	[redacted]

As: Spouse of the deceased.

Given under the seal of the Supreme Court of Queensland

A. R. HAMS

DEPUTY REGISTRAR

29 MAY 2007

GRANT IN PROBATE AND ADMINISTRATION JURISDICTION
Prepared and Filed in the Registry

Form 72

McCULLOUGH ROBERTSON LAWYERS
Level 5 "Central Plaza II"
66 Eagle Street
BRISBANE QLD 4000

WHY

1. Financial institution requirements
2. Property transfers
3. Concern about potential claim against will
4. Protection for executor

ADMINISTRATION PROCESS

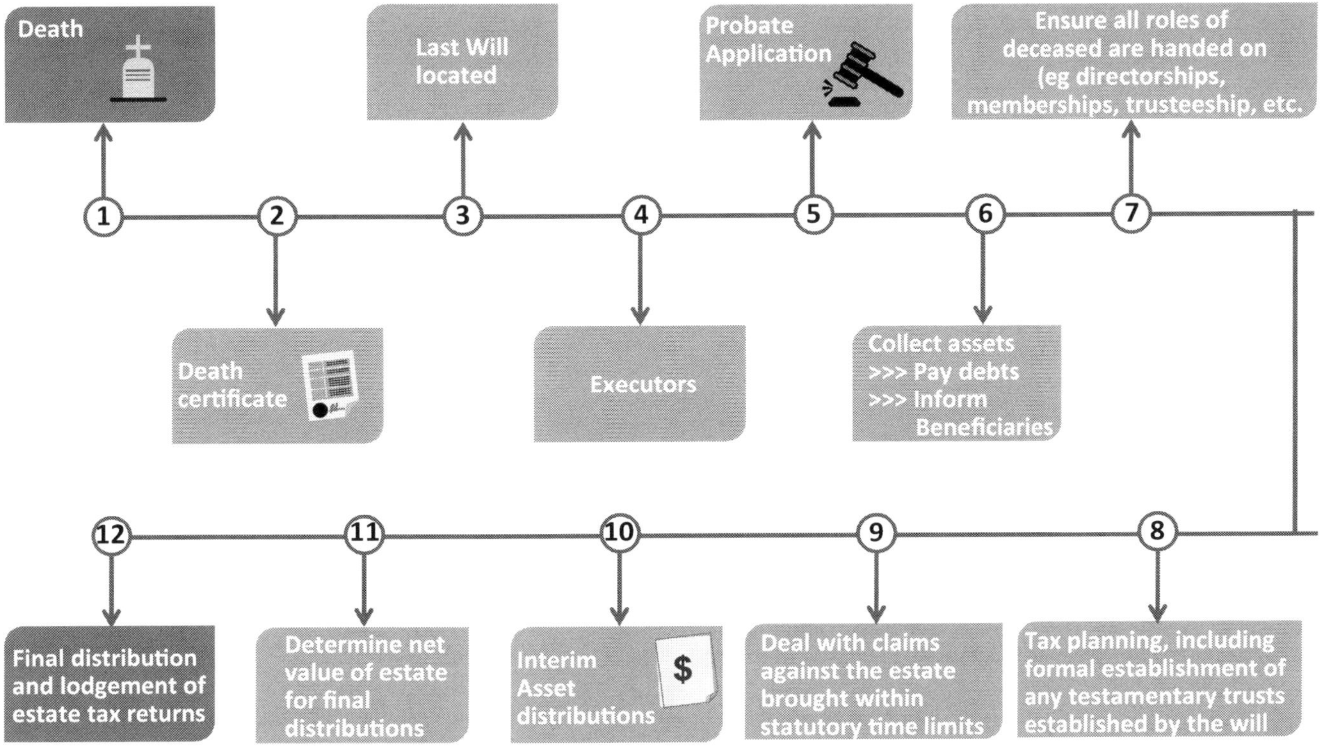

DOCUMENTS TO BE SUBMITTED

Original will

Original death certificate

Affidavit

Service/ advertising

Statement of assests and liabilities

GRANT OF REPRESENTATION

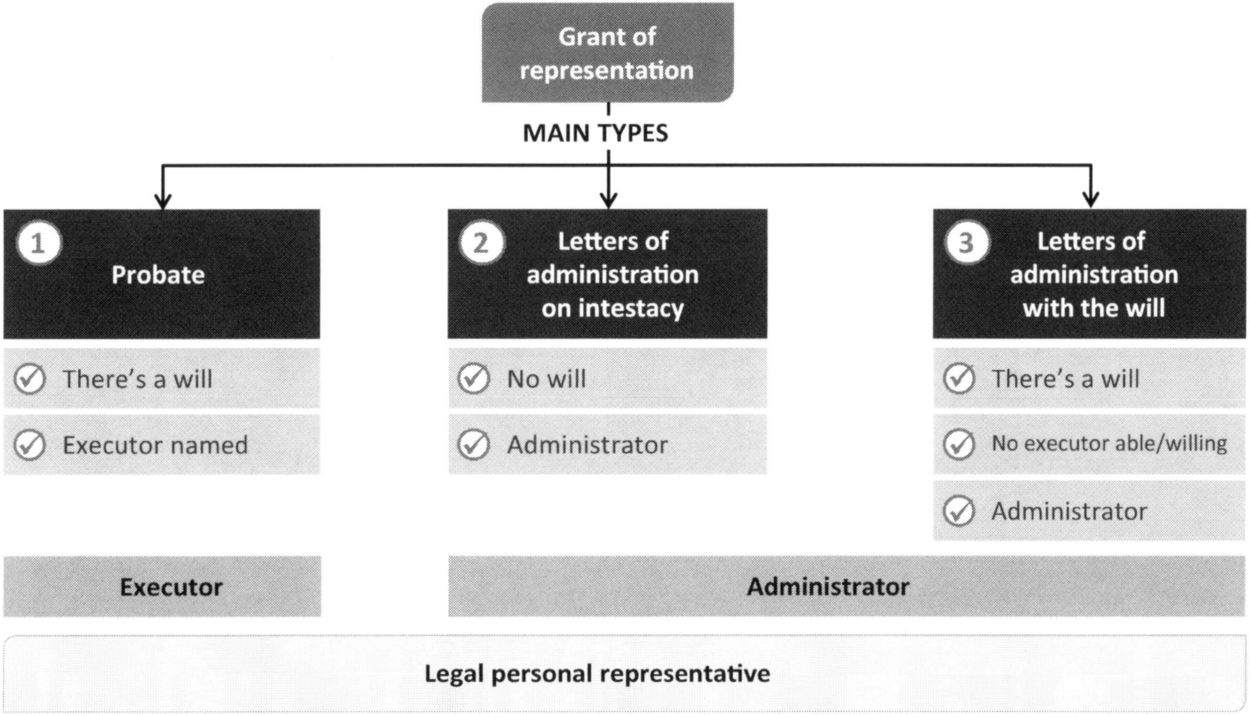

PREREQUISITES

	Probate	Letters of administration with Will
Valid will	✓	✓
Named executor	✓	✓
Executor is willing and able to act	✓	
Executor is unwilling or unable to act		✓
No challenges	✓	✓
Beware of notional estate rules	✓	✓

NOTES

INTESTACY

The intestacy provisions apply where a person dies without a valid will in relation to all of their assets. In this regard, it can in fact be possible to die 'partially intestate'. This simply means that there are assets in a person's estate that are not validly dealt with under the will in place at a person's death.

The intestacy rules are (at least currently) inconsistent across each state in Australia.

The intestacy rules in each state are however set out under the relevant Succession Acts and, in very broad terms, provide for the distribution of wealth amongst immediate family members according to predetermined formulas.

INTESTACY

①	Death without a valid will in place
②	Different rules in each State
③	Administrator
④	Distribution of assets determined by intestacy rules

CHALLENGES

Laws in each state of Australia allow a family member or certain other dependants to challenge a deceased's will. Such a claim is generally known as either an FPA or TFM. Whether a TFM or FPA claim is successful depends upon a range of matters—regardless of the outcome however, TFMs or FPAs can be costly and emotionally debilitating for all parties involved.

There are strict timeframes within which a TFM or FPA can be made.

The five main mechanisms by which a will may be challenged are:

(1) lack of testamentary capacity (i.e. the willmaker did not understand the nature and effect of the document they were signing);
(2) contractual obligations (i.e. it can be shown that the willmaker entered into an arrangement that overrides the provisions of their last will);
(3) a later, inconsistent, testamentary document (i.e. despite a will receiving probate, a later document is discovered that is inconsistent with what was otherwise understood to be the final will);
(4) undue influence (i.e. the willmaker signed a document that they were essentially forced into or misled about its contents);
(5) family provision application (i.e. a person who is within a defined category of relationship with the willmaker challenges the provisions of the will on the basis that the willmaker failed to make adequate provision for the person's proper maintenance and support).

TIMEFRAMES

Notice for FPA – broadly ...

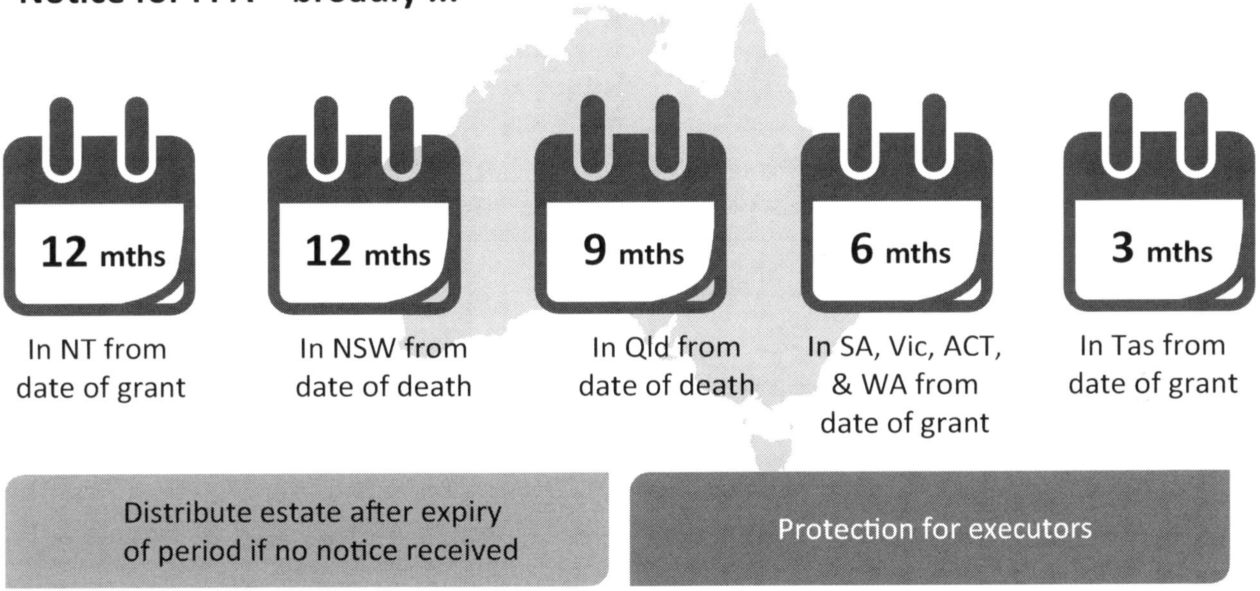

NOTIONAL ESTATES

Historically in all Australian states, a TFM or FPA claim could only relate to property that was owned by the deceased on the date of their death, putting certain property—such as trust assets or those owned by a spouse—outside the reach of a TFM or FPA claim.

In 2005, NSW introduced 'notional estate' provisions, which essentially enable a court to treat certain property that is not legally part of a deceased estate, as being deemed to be included and thereby open to attack by a TFM. These provisions apply to NSW domiciled persons and any property located within NSW.

For property to be part of a notional estate, 'a relevant property transaction' must have occurred, which in broad terms requires a positive act or omission that results in property being owned by someone other than the deceased. The offending transaction must have taken place within certain specified times before the date of death of the willmaker.

NSW NOTIONAL ESTATE

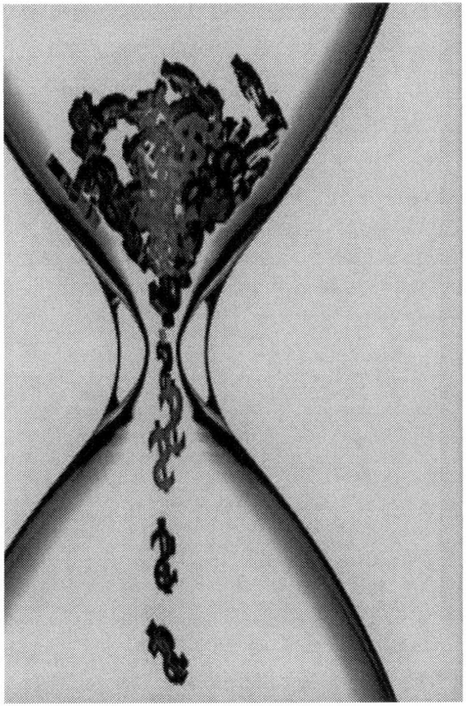

①	Assets in other entities
②	Transfers can be 'clawed' back
③	Joint tenancy
④	Other states
⑤	Super

TAX CONSEQUENCES

Upon death, each asset of the deceased will potentially be transferred three times:

(1) from the deceased to the LPR;
(2) from the LPR to the beneficiary of the estate, which may be the trustee of a TT; and
(3) from the TT to a beneficiary either as a capital distribution during the lifetime of the trust or as a distribution of corpus upon vesting.

The CGT consequences of the first two scenarios outlined above are set out below.

The tax position in relation to the transfer of assets out of a TT to a beneficiary is complex and specific advice should be obtained at the time such a transfer is being considered.

The main transaction costs in the administration of a deceased estate are tax and stamp duty.

Generally, there should be no stamp duty payable for any transfer of assets under a will.

The taxation issues are however more complex, particularly where a testamentary trust is set up under the deceased's will.

It is important to note that capital gains tax should not apply to these assets:

(1) the will-maker's main residence—if it is sold within two years of their death or if it is used by a beneficiary as their main residence under a right in the will (even if sold after two years);
(2) motor vehicles;

(3) personal belongings not exceeding $10,000;

(4) most superannuation and life insurance policies; and

(5) for small business owners, assets where all relevant capital gains tax small business concession conditions are satisfied.

TAXATION MATTERS

① Arrange for lodgement of outstanding tax returns

② Obtain a tax file number for the estate

③ Provide beneficiaries details of income for personal returns

④ Determine costs bases and acquisition dates for CGT assets

⑤ Provide cost base schedules to beneficiaries for future reference

⑥ Consider implications where there are overseas beneficiaries

⑦ Taxation on superannuation death benefits paid to estate

⑧ Final tax return

TAX PLANNING

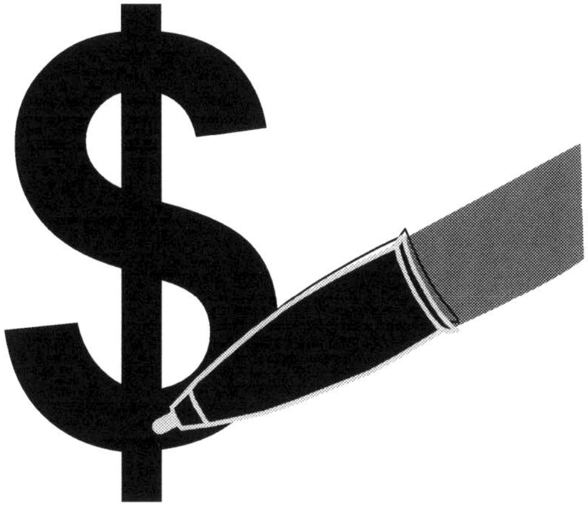

1. Excepted trust income is available via TTs
2. Refinancing loan arrangements and UPEs
3. Division 7A must be on the checklist
4. CGT relief only for transfers under a will
5. Avoiding superannuation death tax

DIVISION 6AA

①

Excepted trust income – sections 102AG(2)(a)(i) and 102AG(2)(d)(i)

②

Minors taxed as adults on distributions from Testamentary Trust

③

Approximately $20,000 tax free and the balance at normal adult rates

④

Excepted trust income is the amount which is assessable income of a trust estate that resulted from a will, codicil or court order varying a will or codicil

EXCEPTED TRUST INCOME

① Super pensions v TTs	② How the tax rules work	③ Grandchildren
④ Managing credit loans as kids reach age of 18	⑤ Trustee duties	⑥ Documentation

DISTRIBUTIONS FROM DECEASED TO LPR

On death, any capital gain or loss from any event relating to a CGT asset owned by the deceased is disregarded. This means that the distribution from the deceased to their LPR does not result in a CGT liability for the deceased.

The LPR is deemed to acquire the assets on the date the deceased died. Broadly the cost base of each CGT asset is:

(1) for pre-CGT assets in the hands of the deceased—the first element of the LPR's cost base (and reduced cost base) is the market value of the asset on the day the deceased died (meaning that pre-CGT assets in the hands of the deceased become post-CGT assets in the hands of the LPR); and

(2) for post-CGT assets in the hands of the deceased—the first element of the LPR's cost base (and reduced cost base) is the deceased's cost base (or reduced cost base) at the date of their death (i.e. the deceased effectively passes their cost base and reduced cost base to the LPR).

DISTRIBUTIONS FROM LPR TO A TESTAMENTARY TRUST

The CGT rules which apply to the distribution from the deceased to the LPR apply in the same manner to subsequent distributions from the LPR to a 'beneficiary' of the estate.

Again, the trustee of the TT is taken to have acquired the CGT assets of the deceased at the date of the deceased's death (rather than on the date they were distributed by the LPR) and the first element of the cost base (and reduced cost base) for the TT trustee will also be:

(1) for pre-CGT assets in the hands of the deceased—the market value of the asset on the day the deceased died; and
(2) for post-CGT assets in the hands of the deceased—the deceased's costs base (or reduced cost base) at the date of their death.

TRIGGER POINTS—SIMPLE WILL

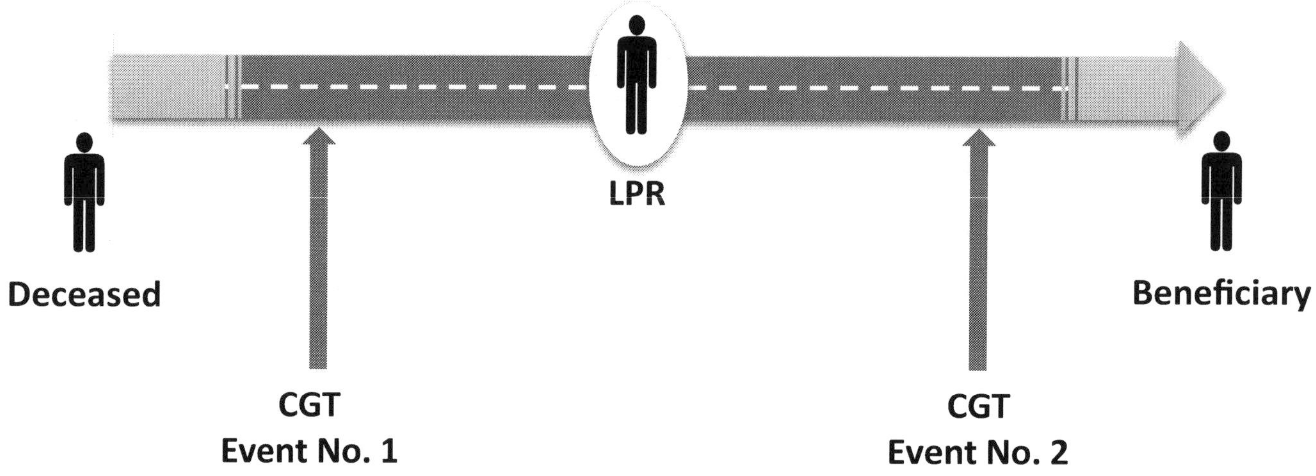

TRIGGER POINTS—TESTAMENTARY TRUSTS

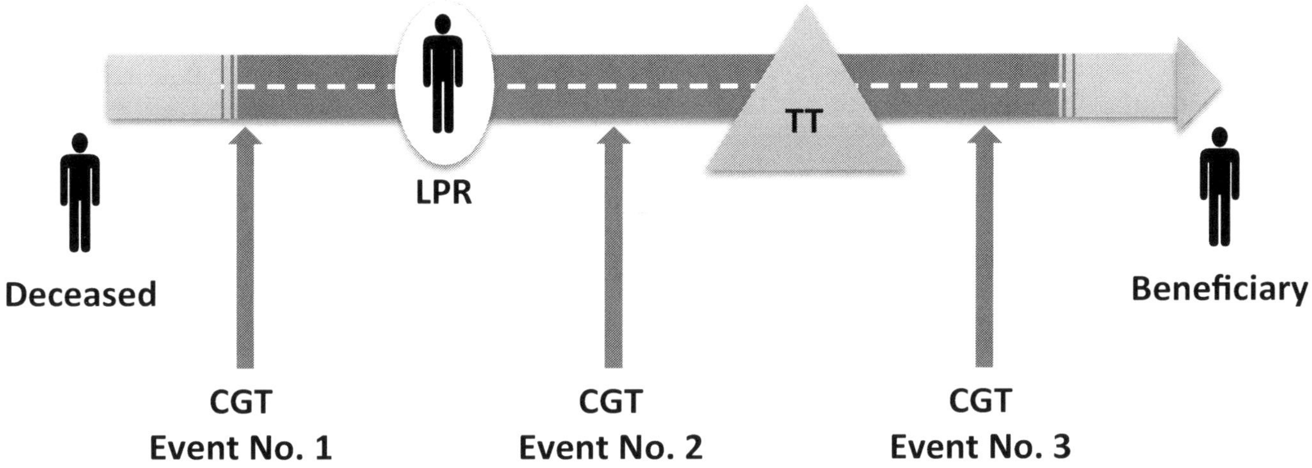

COMPANY ASSETS

Any assets owned by a private company will continue to be owned by the company following the death of an individual shareholder.

There are however 3 key aspects that an executor should be aware of in relation to private companies a deceased had shares in at the date of death, namely:

(1) what happens to the shares;
(2) debts owed to the deceased; and
(3) debts owed by the deceased.

Each of the above issues are dealt with in turn below.

WHAT HAPPENS TO COMPANY SHARES OWNED BY THE DECEASED ON DEATH?

Unlike a trust, a company is a separate legal entity. It has its own legal identity that is discrete from the shareholders.

Companies can own property, enter into contracts and be subject to legal liability in the same manner as an ordinary person.

Shares represent ownership of a company. However, even as owner, a shareholder is not entitled to the assets of the company. Thus, the death of a shareholder has no effect on the company's continuing existence.

However, the shares owned by the deceased in a company form part of their estate assets and can be disposed of by their will.

During the period when the deceased's estate is being administered, their executor will be able to exercise any rights that attach to their shares—for example, voting at general meetings.

DEBTS OWED TO THE DECEASED BY A COMPANY

A company can often owe money to its shareholders. This may arise, for example, if shareholders lend the dividends they earn back to the company.

This sum then becomes an asset of the deceased, separate from the shares themselves.

The executor will be responsible for calling in the relevant debt to be administered in accordance with the will, or otherwise negotiating, for example, the forgiveness of the debt.

There are a range of potential tax and stamp duty consequences that the executor will need to take into account when calling in or negotiating the debt.

DEBTS OWED BY THE DECEASED TO A COMPANY

A debt owed by a deceased to a company ordinarily causes a 'debit' loan account to arise.

There are several potential tax consequences when dealing with the debt (particularly under the deemed dividend rules in Division 7A of the Tax Act).

Practically, subject to managing the tax issues, any debt owed by a deceased to a company, on death may be dealt with by the executor by being:

(1) repaid by the estate;
(2) forgiven; or
(3) allowed to form part of the estate, with the obligation to repay passing to one or more beneficiaries.

Again, there are a range of potential tax and stamp duty consequences that the executor will need to take into account in relation to any debts owed by the deceased and generally specialist advice should be obtained.

CONTROL OF COMPANIES

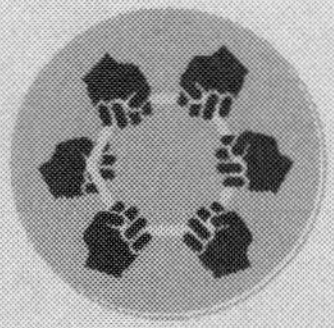

Share rights

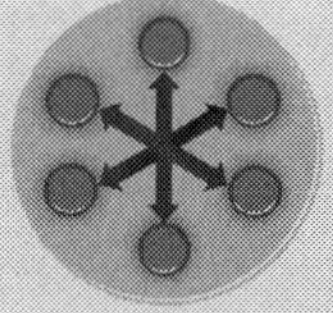

Allotments

Tax

Duty

Corps Act

SHAREHOLDER AGREEMENTS

① Framework

② Board succession

③ Voting rights

④ Pre-emption

⑤ Takeover

⑥ Drag along

SUPERANNUATION

A person's superannuation benefits might not form part of their estate and are often dealt with at the discretion of the superannuation fund's trustee, depending on the fund's trust deed.

There are a multitude of complex issues surrounding superannuation generally, particularly on death.

Set out below is a summary of some of the key issues on the death of a member, however it is strongly recommended that the executor obtain specialist advice prior to any payments being made, at least in relation to the proposed payment of superannuation entitlements and the tax consequences.

WHO ARE ELIGIBLE RECIPIENTS OF SUPERANNUATION BENEFITS ON DEATH?

A superannuation fund trustee may only pay a superannuation death benefit to a deceased member's 'dependant', or their legal personal representative.

The term 'dependant' has its ordinary meaning of someone who was receiving and relying on financial support from the deceased at the time of their death. Superannuation legislation extends the term 'dependant' to include any of the following, even if they were not receiving financial support from the deceased:

(1) the deceased's spouse—including a legal spouse, de facto at the time of death and a same sex partner;
(2) a child of the deceased—including a natural child, an adopted child, a stepchild (while his or her natural parent is alive) and an ex-nuptial child. The child can be any age; and
(3) any person with whom the deceased had an 'interdependency relationship' at the time of their death.

Importantly, the definition of a dependant for tax purposes is narrower than the above definition. The tax paid on distributions to a non-tax dependant is greater than payments to tax dependants.

THE ROLE OF THE SUPER FUND TRUSTEE

In administering a superannuation fund, a trustee is normally given a number of discretionary powers.

It is generally up to the trustee of the relevant fund to determine whether a person's superannuation benefits are paid to a dependant directly or to their estate. The trustee of the fund may pay the superannuation benefits directly to a person's dependants, and thus bypass the estate.

It is also possible for the moneys to pass through the estate and be dealt with by the will.

The trustee may also have the discretion to determine how those benefits will be paid—either by lump sum or income stream, or possibly a combination of both (although if a benefit is to be paid from a superannuation fund to the estate it can only be paid in the form of a lump sum).

PAYMENT RULES

Essentially a member of a superannuation fund has four main choices for specifying what should happen in relation to their superannuation entitlements on death (assuming the proposed recipient is entitled, as set out above), namely:

(1) no nomination—the trustee of the superannuation fund is bound to deal with a member's benefit in their best interests. Before making a decision, the trustee will normally make enquiries of the executor as to the member's family situation, who their dependants are, the provisions of their will and other relevant circumstances;

(2) a non-BDBN—the trustee is not bound by a non-BDBN and has an absolute discretion as to where the death benefit will be paid. Where a non-BDBN is made, it should be taken into account as part of any decision by the trustee as to how to distribute the benefit;

(3) a BDBN—the trustee is obliged to distribute a member's death benefits in accordance with a valid BDBN; and

(4) a reversionary pension—generally the trustee of a superannuation fund will be required to continue to pay a pension to the person the deceased nominated as any reversionary pensioner.

WHO CAN BENEFIT?

Eligible recipients	Death benefit dependants
LPR	Spouse or former spouse
Dependant (spouse, child or 'interdependency' relationship	Child under 18
	Interdependency relationship
	Financial dependant (under 25)

LUMP SUMS

Relationship	Tax free component	Taxable component (taxed element)	Taxable component (untaxed element)
Dependant or LPR	Tax free	Tax free	Tax free
Non-dependant	Tax free	15% plus Medicare levy	30% plus Medicare levy

PENSIONS

Member	Beneficiary	Tax free component	Taxable component (Taxed element)	Taxable component (Untaxed element
60+	60+	Tax free	Tax free	Marginal rate
60+	<60	N/A	Marginal rate	N/A
<60	60+	Tax free	Tax free	Marginal rate
<60	<60	Tax free	Marginal rate	Marginal rate

SUPERANNUATION WILL

1. Embedded in deed
2. Strict compliance required by trustee
3. Prohibition on amendment
4. Won't generally override a reversionary pension

SPECIFIC ISSUES

While there is a myriad of specific issues to be aware of, 6 of the more common issues that arise as part of a deceased estate are profiled in the following pages.

SPECIFIC TIPS

1. Post death TTs
2. Full names and aliases
3. Contingent and specific gifts
4. Capacity
5. Missing wills
6. Using existing structures

POST DEATH TESTAMENTARY TRUSTS

1. When assets must pass
2. Superannuation proceeds
3. Insurance proceeds
4. Stamp duty implications
5. Excepted trust income to extent of entitlement in the event of intestacy

WHY USE AN EPT?

①	Concessional tax treatment of income
②	Ability to split income—income can be used to pay for education, living and other expenses for children
③	Income taxed at adult rates rather than the penalty rates that normally apply to minors unearned income (access to tax free threshold)
④	Asset protection

HOW DOES IT WORK?

① Death benefits paid to estate

② Within three years, the EPT is established to hold assets received from a deceased estate

③ Trustee makes distributions to the minor children which are taxed at adult marginal rates as excepted trust income

④ The children may be absolutely entitled to their share of capitalonce they turn 18

⑤ Beneficiaries

- Can have a single trust or separate trusts for each child
- Children must be capital beneficiaries
- Can have additional income beneficiaries

EXAMPLE

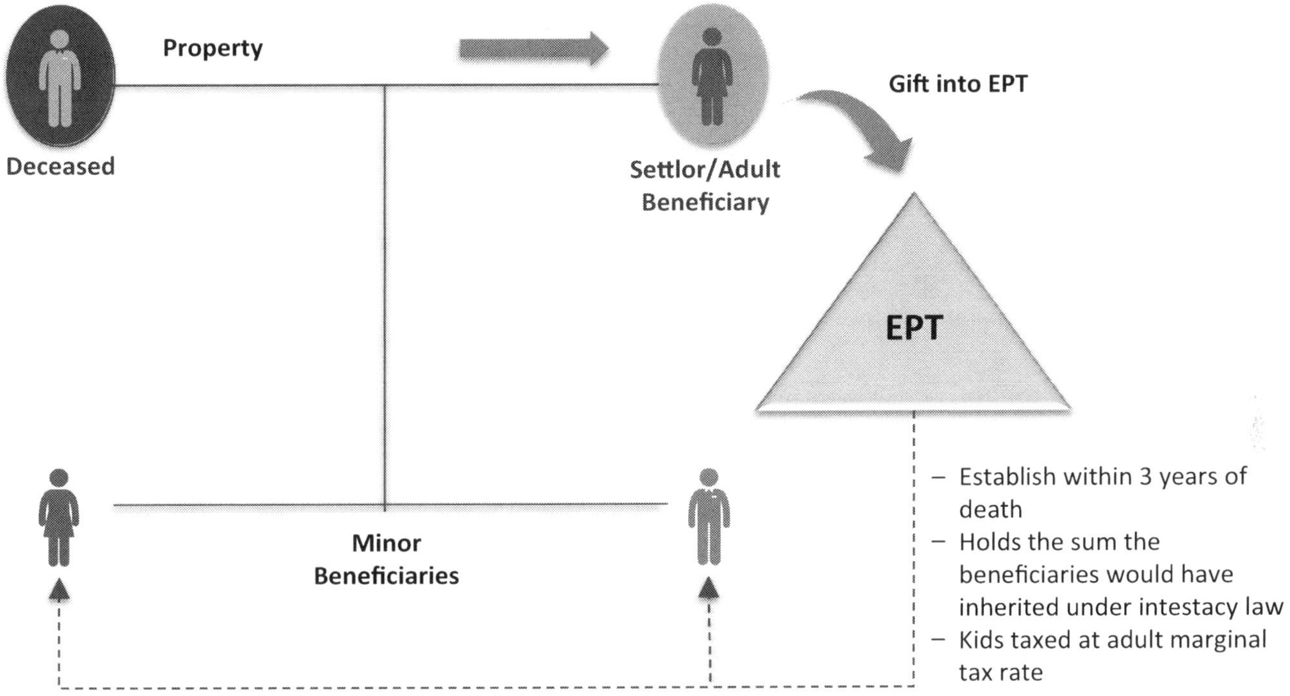
Property
Deceased
Settlor/Adult Beneficiary
Gift into EPT
EPT
Minor Beneficiaries
– Establish within 3 years of death
– Holds the sum the beneficiaries would have inherited under intestacy law
– Kids taxed at adult marginal tax rate

WHAT IS AN SPT

1. Can be established in the will or after the death of the member
2. Established solely for superannuation proceeds
3. Interplay of legislation critical
4. Nominations also important

HOW DOES IT WORK?

1. An SPT can be set up proactively through a TT established under a will
2. Many provide this as a standard
3. BDBN needs to be taken into account
4. Beneficiaries must be death benefit dependants at date of payment

WHO CAN BENEFIT?

① Beneficiaries limited to dependants of the deceased at the date of payment

② Death benefit tax dependant:

- spouse or former spouse of the deceased
- child, under the age of 18, of the deceased
- child, under the age of 25 who is financially dependent on the deceased
- person with whom the deceased had an 'interdependency relationship' with as defined under the *Income Tax Assessment Act 1997*
- any other person financially dependant on the deceased

EXAMPLE

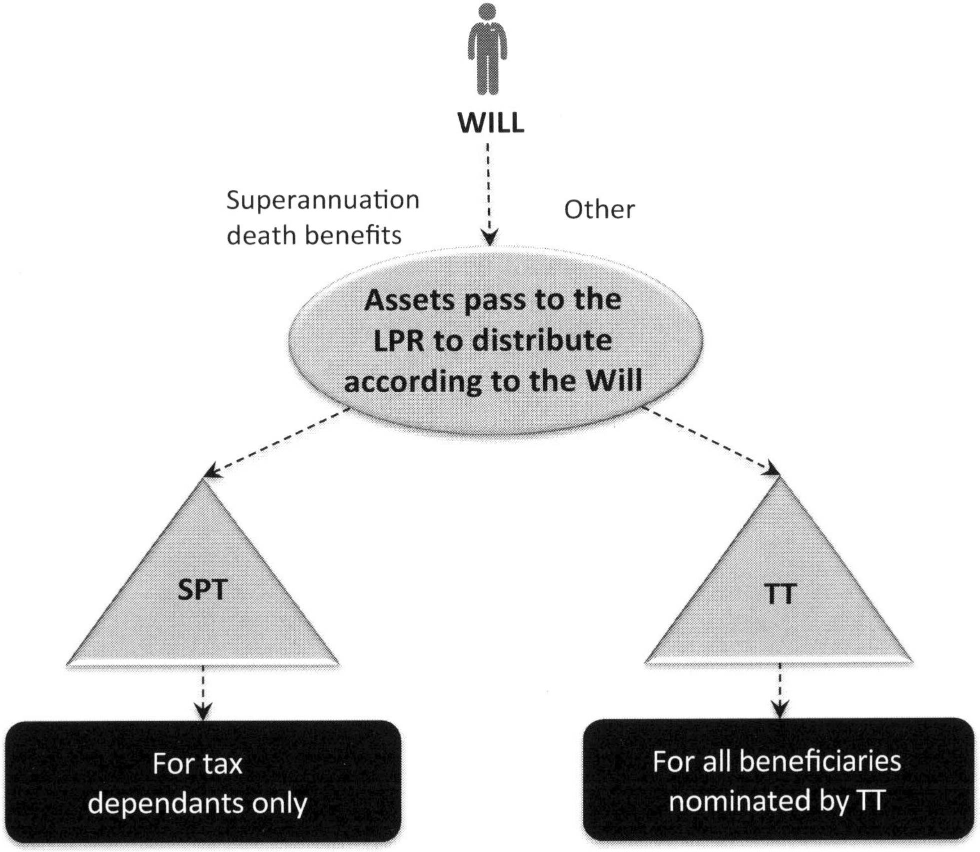

WILL
Superannuation
death benefits
Other
Assets pass to the
LPR to distribute
according to the Will
SPT
TT
For tax
dependants only
For all beneficiaries
nominated by TT

ALIASES

① In the will of 'Matthew William Burgess'

② Death certificate registered with 'William Matthew Burgess'

③ Grant of representation (Advertising, Affidavit of executors)

④ All documents should reference 'both' names …

⑤ … and any other names

⑥ Solution—checklist approach

CONTINGENT GIFTS

① 'Provided she does not challenge my will, I give my daughter $100,000'

② Beware that many contingent gifts will be at risk of being held void

③ Often 'The Vibe' will be applied by court

SPECIFIC GIFTS

① Get the details 100% right

② Beware that will is at risk if gift disposed of

③ Pre-empt sale of gift, by also gifting sale proceeds

④ Use MoD as far as possible

⑤ Ideal outcome = no specific gifts

INCAPACITY

1. Sound mind, memory and understanding
2. Requirements of testator
3. There should be no disorder of the mind and no insane delusions in influencing the disposing of the estate
4. Lucid intervals—can be ok ...

REQUIREMENTS OF WILLMAKER

① Understand the nature of making a will and its effects

② Understand the extent of the property of which the willmaker is disposing

③ Comprehend and appreciate the claims to which the willmaker 'ought' to give effect

LOSS OF CAPACITY

1. Increasingly litigious area as people live longer
2. Contemporaneous certification of medical specialist recommended
3. Internal record keeping and adviser file notes key as well
4. Appropriate approach—all advisers work collaboratively

MISSING DOCUMENTS

Impact on grant of representation

Presumption of destruction

Plan A, B & C

Avoid court

Solutions

STRATEGIES FOR MISSING DOCUMENTS

① Plan A = find them

② Plan B = see plan A

③ Plan C = find any other evidence

④ Ideally at least find an earlier will

⑤ Need not be in writing—eg iPhone, YouTube and voice recorded wills

USING EXISTING STRUCTURES

① 'I leave my Net Estate to the trustee of [#insert an existing family trust]'

② Beware heritage issues with receiving trust

③ Beware risk of a structure being wound up after will signed

④ Tax and duty implications—more problematic than using a TT

⑤ Beware short vesting dates of receiving structure

⑥ Key solution—get specialist advice + use checklists

NOTES

As noted at the start of the Workbook, the baby boomer generation has caused a 'bubble' at each other stage of their lifecycle, meaning from 2016 for around 30 years there will likely be a jump in death rates and the value of intergenerational wealth transfer.

While the administration of a deceased estate is a heavily regulated area, advisers can successfully facilitate or project manage both probate and estate administration more generally of any deceased estate leveraging adviser centric platforms such as View.

THE FACILITATING ADVISERS ROLE IN THE ADMINISTRATION PROCESS

	Adviser	View
Death certificate issued, current will obtained and instructions submitted to View Legal with an asset schedule	✓	
Advertisement/notice of application for grant		✓
Preparation of the application for grant and submission with the court		✓
Grant issued and supplied to adviser		✓
Distribution of assets	✓	(if needed)
Future investment advice	✓	
Facilitating updated estate plans for beneficiaries	✓	✓

ESTATE ADMIN OPPORTUNITIES

- Use estate administration process to widen your client base
- Maintain FUM, otherwise at risk on death of client
- Intergenerational advice opportunities—administration of the estate and advice to beneficiaries
- Satisfy compliance obligations
- Perfect complementary solution to front end estate planning
- Diversified offering that can be delivered on a fee for service basis

ONGOING VALUE ADDS

① Financing arrangements	② Securitisation and asset protection	③ Structure simplification (especially arrangements of a surviving spouse)
④ Complementary control of related entities (e.g. principal/appointor etc.)	⑤ Planning advice where multiple families are part of a single TT	⑥ Distributions to and from existing family trusts

ADVISER AS EXECUTORS

①	Professional indemnity
②	More than just investments
③	Unknown unknowns
④	Conflicts
⑤	Professional charging clauses

CALLS TO ACTION

NOTES

Chapter 3

Assets and Liabilities Checklist

NOTES

A summary of the assets and liabilities that may need to be considered as part of the administration of a deceased estate is set out below.

The table is not intended to be an exhaustive list of the assets and liabilities that may need to be considered as part of the administration of a deceased estate.

Rather it is provided to highlight the importance for clients to work with all their advisers including their financial planner, accountant, lawyer and insurance adviser in any estate administration exercise.

	Category	Description	Location	Estimated Value	Comments
ASSETS					
1.	Real estate	[#Detail of address of each property and real property description] (n.b. any rent received)		$	
2.	Leasehold (including crown leases)	[#Details of lease]		$	
3.	Water allocation	[#Detail of allocation. Consider whether relevant to land which is subject to specific gift or whether forms part of the residuary]		$	
4.	Bank accounts	[#Details of institution, account number, account name for each account, balance at date of death]		$	
5.	Cash	[#Details of any money in hand]		$	
6.	Investments (including options)			$	

	Category	Description	Location	Estimated Value	Comments
7.	Shares in publicly listed companies	[#Details of number of shares, name of company, calls outstanding and type of share for each shareholding etc.]		$	
8.	Units in public unit trusts	[#Details of units held, trust and trustee]		$	
9.	Securities and bonds	[#Details]		$	
10.	Debentures, secured and unsecured notes	[#Details]		$	
11.	Entities			$	
12.	Companies	[#Number of shares, type of shares, name of company, ABN number and office held in company, if any, e.g. director]		$	
13.	Trusts	[#Name of trust, nature of trust, trustee, interest held in trust, e.g. beneficiary (indicate class of beneficiary)/principal etc. and any powers (e.g. property of which the deceased had a power of appointment)]		$	
14.	Interests in partnerships and joint ventures	[#Name of partnership, share (e.g. %) and interest held (in capital and income)]		$	
15.	Sole proprietorship	[#Name of business and details of stock in trade and goodwill]		$	
16.	Farm interest	[#Including details of livestock, crops, farming implements, machinery and saddlery]		$	

	Category	Description	Location	Estimated Value	Comments
17.	Life insurance policies	[#Details of insurance company, policy number, type of policy and beneficiary for each life policy, current surrender value of policy]		$	
18.	Debt due to the deceased (Note: search the PPSR)	[#Details of unpaid wages or any loan which is due to the deceased (by third parties or entities), including monies due under a mortgage, bill of sale or promissory note]		$	
19.	An interest in another deceased's person's estate	[#Details of the other deceased's person's estate and nature of the interest]		$	
20.	Compensation	[#Details of any compensation entitlement (e.g. for personal injury), type of payment received (e.g. lump sum) and amount received]		$	
21.	Furniture, chattels and whitegoods	[#Provide detailed inventory of furniture including antiques, heirlooms, whitegoods, electricals, silverware and other contents—attach copy]		$	
22.	Jewellery	[#Description]		$	
23.	Artwork	[#Name of artist and painting of each piece of work]		$	
24.	Wine cellar	[#Inventory of wine]		$	
25.	Stamp, coin and/or other collection of valuables	[#Catalogue of collection]		$	
26.	Motor vehicles	[#Detail of year, make, model and registration number of each vehicle]		$	

	Category	Description	Location	Estimated Value	Comments
27.	Boats	[#Detail of type of boat and present mooring]		$	
28.	Digital Assets	[#Details]		$	
29.	Refunds			$	
30.	Private health insurance	[#Details of insurer and membership number]		$	
31.	Funeral expense contribution	[#Details, consider private health insurance and Department of Veteran Affairs]		$	
32.	Pre-paid funeral plan	[#Details of pre-paid funeral plan]		$	
33.	Car insurance	[#Details of insurer and membership number]		$	
34.	House insurance	[#Details of insurer and membership number]		$	
35.	Medicare	[#Medicare number]		$	
36.	Motoring club	[#Details of club and membership number]		$	
37.	Tax refund—date of death return	[#Details]		$	
38.	Tax refund—estate return	[#Details]		$	
39.	Other property and interests	[#Details of overseas assets/Managed investment scheme interests/ Holiday or country club entitlements]		$	
TOTAL ASSETS:				$	

	Category	Description	Location	Estimated Value	Comments
LIABILITIES					
40.	Credit card accounts	[#Details of credit provider, account number, limit and balance at date of death]		$	
41.	Loans owed by deceased at date of death			$	
42.	Secured debts (mortgages and other personal loans)	[Search PPSR and obtain appropriate releases. #Detail of institution or person, type of loan (e.g. housing loan), account number and security, e.g. over home]		$	
43.	Overdraft Facilities	[#Detail of institution and account number]		$	
44.	Leases, hire purchase and other credit facilities	[#Detail of institution, type of facility and account number]		$	
45.	Unsecured loans	[#Details]		$	
46.	Litigation	[#Details of any actions against the deceased]		$	
47.	Miscellaneous			$	
48.	Medical/hospital account	[#Details]		$	
49.	Funeral account	[#Details]		$	
50.	Domestic account	[#Details]		$	
51.	Rates/utilities	[#Details]		$	
52.	Taxation liability at date of death	[#Details]		$	

	Category	Description	Location	Estimated Value	Comments
53.	Other liabilities (including contingent liabilities)	[#Details]		$	
TOTAL LIABILTIES:				$	
NET ESTATE:				$	
NON-ESTATE ASSETS AND LIABILITIES					
54.	Superannuation	[#Name of superannuation fund, name of trustee, interest held in fund, nominations in place and type of nomination]		$	
55.	Private schemes	[#Name of institution, membership or account number and surrender value]		$	
56.	Other entitlements	[#Details]		$	

Chapter 4

Estate Administration Checklist

NOTES

The below table sets out the suggested steps in relation to the administration of the estate of the Deceased. All timeframes are a guide only and may vary depending on third parties.

Item	Action Item	Comments	Timeframe
1	Notifications	We recommend that you write to any banks where the Deceased held funds to freeze accounts. You should also write to any relevant entities to cancel memberships, direct debit payments and to the electoral office to cancel the Deceased's enrolment. If the Deceased was in receipt of any pension payments, we suggest the relevant organisations be notified to cancel the pension payments.	Immediately
2	Identification of assets	Only assets owned by the deceased personally form part of their estate, to be administered by the executor. There are a wide range of assets that generally do not form part of a deceased estate. A complete list of the assets and liabilities of the Deceased should be compiled. A schedule of items that should be considered is attached.	Within 6 weeks from the date of death
3	Death certificate	A death certificate is required to obtain probate of the will of the Deceased (Will). A standard death certificate shows the full details of the death record and is a recognised identity document that informs government agencies and financial institutions that a person has passed away. [#delete if already obtained]Most of the time you will not need to apply for a death certificate, the funeral director will apply for a standard death certificate on your behalf when you organise the funeral. If you require an additional or replacement death certificate, an application can be made to the Registry for Births, Deaths, and Marriages. [#delete if not relevant]If the person passed away outside Australia, contact the Registry for Births, Deaths, and Marriages to get advice on how to get a copy of the death certificate.	6 weeks from the date of death

Item	Action Item	Comments	Timeframe
4	Probate	[#Option 1: if probate application is not yet being prepared]Applying for and receiving probate of the Will broadly requires the following steps: (a) Publication of a notice of intention to apply for a grant of probate; (b) Lodgement of the 'tear sheet' proving the advertisement with the Public Trustee; (c) Signing of the application for grant of probate and supporting documents; (d) Filing of the application for grant of probate and supporting documents with the Supreme Court of Queensland; and (e) Receiving the grant of probate from the Supreme Court of Queensland.[#end option] [Option 2: if probate application is already being prepared]As you know, steps are being taken to lodge an application for probate of the Will.[#end option]	[#Option 1: if probate application is not yet being prepared]From date of death: (a) 7 weeks (b) 8 weeks (c) 8 weeks (d) 10 weeks (e) 15—20 weeks. [#end option] [Option 2: if probate application is already being prepared]We will update you when we have received confirmation that probate has been granted. [#end option]

Item	Action Item	Comments	Timeframe
5	Financial statements	Contact should be made with the Deceased's accountant to obtain financial statements for the Deceased and any relevant trusts or companies in the Group. In particular, any information relevant to the cost base of the Deceased's shares and investment properties should be obtained in order to confirm the various tax implications of administering the estate. The financial statements should also be reviewed to identify any loans within the Group.	6 weeks from the date of death
6	Joint assets	Action should be taken to commence arrangements for transfer of any assets held jointly by the Deceased and another person. [#check if we have access to ownership of properties]When assets are held as joint tenants, the death of the first joint tenant must be officially recorded with various government departments and financial institutions. For instance: (a) when bank accounts are held in joint names, the bank must be notified of the death of one of the joint holders; (b) when real property is held as joint tenants (i.e. a leasehold or freehold interest in residential or commercial property), the relevant government department must be notified and the change of ownership recorded on the property register; and (c) when shares in a public company are held as joint tenants, the relevant share registry must be notified and ASIC records must be updated for shares in private companies.	6 weeks from the date probate issues
7	Contact Trustees of Testamentary Trusts	Contact should be made with the trustees of each TT established via the Will. In this regard, the trustee of each TT should be provided with a certified copy of the Will. Each trustee should also be advised: (a) of the existence of the TT; and (b) of their duties and responsibilities as a trustee. We recommend you suggest to each trustee to contact us to seek specialist legal advice as soon as practicable in relation to their duties and responsibilities as a trustee.	As soon as practical

Item	Action Item	Comments	Timeframe
8	Contact beneficiaries [#delete if only beneficiaries are executors]	The beneficiaries entitled to receive distributions under the Deceased's Will should be written to. [#if TTs in will]Contact should be made with the trustee of each TT to inform them of the entitlement of the beneficiaries for which they are to hold the share of the Estate on trust for. Any correspondence should generally include a copy of the Will and details regarding the planned course of action in the administration of the Estate.	7 weeks from date of probate
9	Notify entities to enable transfer of assets	We recommend that you write to any banks, superannuation funds, share registries and other relevant entities where the Deceased held assets or funds to request details of their forms and requirements to transfer the assets or funds.	7 weeks from date of probate
10	Tax advice	We recommend you arrange meetings with the following parties: (a) [#check if only advising one executor/only one executor appointed]the other executors; (b) the Deceased's share broker (if any); (c) [#remove if executors are only beneficiaries]beneficiaries of the Estate; and (d) the Deceased's accountant, to discuss management of the Estate generally and specific issues such as capital gains tax and income tax, the manner in which beneficiaries wish to receive their entitlement, any potential appropriation of assets and formal establishment of [#any/the] TT.	14 weeks from date of probate
11	Asset sale	If assets are to be sold as opposed to transferred to beneficiaries, steps should be taken to commence the sale process. This may also involve collecting cash proceeds into a trust account established for the purpose of administering the Estate. Any funds held in trust should be invested in an interest-bearing bank account until final distribution to the beneficiaries.	20 weeks from date of probate

Item	Action Item	Comments	Timeframe
12	Credit releases	As soon as relevant funds become available, the remaining debts of the Deceased should be settled. The release of any mortgage over property should also be implemented. Where appropriate, repayment of any loans owing to any entities in the Group should be made.	When funds available
13	Administration accounts	We recommend preparation of draft administration accounts by the deceased's accountant for review by the executors [#delete if only beneficiaries are executors]before being sent to the beneficiaries.	20 weeks from date of probate
14	Tax return—Deceased	A tax return for the Deceased should be prepared by the Deceased's accountant.	20 weeks from date of probate
15	Control of entities	The succession of any role of control held by the Deceased (e.g. trustee, appointor/principal, director or secretary) of an entity in the Group should be implemented. Documents should be prepared to effect the change of those roles and lodged with ASIC, OSR, Titles Office or other relevant body (as appropriate).	20 weeks from date of probate
16	Transfer assets to TT [#check if TTs in Will]	The relevant assets of the Estate to be transferred to the [#trustee/s] of [#any/the] TT established via the Will should be progressed. Care should be taken to ensure the correct assets are transferred[#check if relevant] and that any superannuation funds that are to pass to a TT are quarantined where there is potential for a 'sub trust' for tax purposes. If there is a property to be transferred to a testamentary trust that will be used as a main residence for tax purposes, specific tax advice should be obtained as to how to best structure the arrangements (including, for example, the trustee resolving to create an express right to occupy).	20 weeks from date of probate
17	Update beneficiaries [#delete if only beneficiaries are executors]	We recommend writing to the beneficiaries [#and any trustees of TTs] to update them on the administration of the Estate. Any communication should seek to confirm their preferences about the manner in which they wish to receive their entitlement and the anticipated income tax and capital gains tax consequences.	20 weeks from date of probate

Item	Action Item	Comments	Timeframe
18	Administration accounts update	We recommend continued liaising with institutions in the collection of the assets. This includes ensuring the Deceased's accountant updates the administration accounts [#delete if only beneficiaries are executors]and providing the updated accounts to the beneficiaries.	17–24 weeks from date of probate
19	Distribute to beneficiaries	No distributions should be made if there is notice that a FPA has been received. For clarity, where a family member, spouse, or dependent of the Deceased is unhappy with their entitlements under the Will, they can approach the court to review the terms of the Will. This is referred to as a 'family provision application'. If an FPA is to occur, the executor will receive a letter. We recommend you contact us to seek specialist legal advice as soon as practical if you receive this type of letter.	6 months from date of death
20	Continue distribution	Assuming no FPA is made, further advancements of the assets to the beneficiaries can be made. [#delete if only beneficiaries are executors]We recommend periodical updating of the administration accounts and provision of these to the beneficiaries.	7–12 months from date of death
21	Tax Return—Estate	Tax returns for the Estate should be prepared by the Deceased's accountant for each year the Estate is in existence.	With 3 months of the end of each tax year
22	Final distribution	If no FPA is made, final distributions of the assets to the beneficiaries should be made following receipt of the final tax assessment. [#delete if only beneficiaries are executors]We recommend a letter be provided to each of the beneficiaries that includes: (a) the final administration accounts have been prepared by the Deceased's accountant; (b) another copy of the Will; and (c) confirmation that administration of the Estate has now been completed.	Within 8 weeks of final tax assessment

Acknowledgement

This book is the result of contributions from a number of people, each of whom I thank.

In particular:

(1) The team I work with at View Legal, provide an environment dedicated to continual improvement. Our sharing of knowledge as a team is reflected by the sharing of knowledge, example being this publication – being only one of many.

(2) All members inspire me to do better each day, and particularly thank you goes to Naomi Arnold, Patrick Ellwood and Tara Lucke for constantly raising our standards from a legal perspective.

(3) Finally, thank you to my family, for being on this journey with me.

Interested to learn more?

View has invested heavily to help advisers help their clients.
Some popular examples of our adviser tools are as follows:

1. **Subscribe to the free weekly blog posts:**

   http://blog.viewlegal.com.au/?m=1

   To subscribe to the blog, simply enter your email address in the subscription box in the right hand column or alternatively, subscribe through your preferred RSS feed from your browser.

2. **View Intellectual Property platform (VIP)**

   The VIP subscription platform provides you with free access to our webinars, as well as preferred pricing access to our books, entity establishment, superannuation and estate planning solutions.

   Even if you trial the VIP platform to update your own estate planning and structuring arrangements it represents fantastic value.

   Learn more at—

   http://viewlegal.com.au/view-vip-subscription-platform-2/

3. **Education programs**

   View Legal specialises in all forms of adviser education and collaborative learning.

   We are fortunate to regularly present to accountants, financial planners, other lawyers and risk advisers.

   Our programs are tailored to meet your specific requirements and can be delivered in lengths ranging from 20 minute web-based updates to 5 day in-house courses (and every permutation in between) and formats including in person, webinar and video streaming. Our most popular sessions tend to be 90 minute team trainings, which can be recorded for future use.

A sample of some of our current topics is set out at the following link—

http://viewlegal.com.au/product-category/events/

Or simply stream or purchase DVD copies of previous programs via the following link—

http://viewlegal.com.au/recorded-webinars/

4. Business model iteration

Matthew Burgess has been recognised as a thought leader in delivery of professional service solutions by peers, industry commentators and competitors. He regularly presents keynotes in this area as well as coordinating and facilitating firm retreats and education programs.

Indeed, Matthew is the only practising lawyer in Australia who is a Certified Speaking Professional (CSP), a designation conferred by the Professional Speakers Australia (PSA), the industry's leading organisation. The CSP is likewise the speaking profession's international measure of professional platform competence.

Matthew is counted among the rare 12 percent of professional speakers worldwide who currently hold the CSP credential.

Learn more about Matthew's business model presentations here—

https://viewlegal.com.au/matthewburgessspeaking/

Learn more about the 3 business books Matthew has written here—

http://www.thedreamenabler.com.au/

A Selection of Other Books from View Legal

For all the latest books please visit https://viewlegal.com.au/product-category/books/

About View

At View Legal our mantra is to be 'for friends'.

In other words, creating solutions and value propositions that are compelling to our friends.

To achieve our vision, we have set out to fundamentally and radically revolutionise access to high quality legal advice, in our areas of deep specialisation—structuring, tax, trusts, asset protection, business sales, estate and succession planning.

To help explain the approach View is taking to uniquely deliver valuable legal solutions, the following table lists 10 traditional ways law firms have operated (and, almost exclusively, continue to operate) and the new vision that View is built around.

Old view	View Legal
Bill clients on hourly rates (or various, increasingly elaborate, permutations on the theme) and have no particular interest in client perception of value	Customers provided up front 'SPS Guarantee'—that is service and price satisfaction is guaranteed with all work undertaken following upfront fixed pricing
Everything tracked on a timesheet. The longer something takes, the better	No timesheets. Sophisticated project management tools used to help ensure customer expectations are exceeded
Quality is defined by the law firm	Quality is defined by the customer
'Impressive' CBD office space, with 'dominant' fit outs	View meets where best suits customers. No permanent CBD space retained
Intellectual property is how we make money and should be guarded jealously	Intellectual property is how we create trust and should be shared freely
Lawyers striving to deliver near-perfect technical excellence	All service designed to be fit-for-purpose, aligning with collaboratively agreed customer objectives
Lawyers cultural focus on 'is this billable' for the firm	Lawyers cultural focus on 'is this valuable' for the customer
'Leveraging' of full-time lawyers to do the bulk of the work serving clients	Flexible work practices that match supply with demand
Constant focus on the 'need for diversity' of gender	Only focus on diversity of thought
Revenue growth the #1 goal	Exceeding customer expectations #1 goal

Significant inspiration provided by VeraSage. Partly adapted with permission of George Beaton, Beaton Capital.

If you would like to learn more about any of the above solutions or View more generally contact 1300 View 00 (1300 843 900), email mail@viewlegal.com.au or contact one of the founders listed at the foot of our home page at—http://viewlegal.com.au/

About the Author

Matthew Burgess is one of the founders of specialist firm View Legal.

Having the opportunity to help clients achieve their goals is what he is most passionate about.

As Matthew always works in conjunction with trusted advisers (whether it be accountants, financial advisers or other lawyers) and their clients, finding ways to fundamentally improve the value received by those advisers, and in turn their clients, has led him to develop numerous game changing models. Examples include providing guaranteed upfront fixed pricing, founding what is widely regarded as Australia's first virtual law firm, and more recently, developing a platform that gives advisers access to market leading advice and support for less than $1 a week.

Matthew's specialisation in tax, structuring, asset protection, estate and succession planning has seen him recognised by most leading industry associations including the Tax Institute, the Weekly Tax Bulletin and in the 2014 'Best Lawyers' list for trusts and estates and either personally, or as part of View, since 2015 in 'Doyles' for taxation and since 2017 for wills, estates and succession planning.

Work is one aspect of his life Matthew loves, so there is no need to be constantly searching for 'balance'. His other great loves are:

(1) Family—they are profiled in various ways through the series of children's books he has written under the pseudonym 'Lily Burgess'—see www.wordsfromdaddysmouth.com.au and various TV commercials;

(2) Learning—going cold Turkey on television and most forms of media in late 2005 has radically increased Matthew's ability to study the great authors and inspired him to publish a series of books that explore the concept of 'true success'—see www.thedreamenabler.com.au

(3) Health—aside from being a foodie and swimming at least a 5km a week, Matthew installed a stand up workstation in 2007 and among a few other lifestyle choices, it changed his life.

Testimonials

A selection of testimonials for presentations by View (including for organisations such as The Tax Institute, various law societies, Television Education Network, AMP, NAB and ALPMA) are as follows:

> Excellent session. Full of interactivity and practical examples/cases.

> I wanted to send you a quick note to say that I thought the session you presented was superb and certainly in my top 2 for the entire event.

> Your session was the one that we were able to take away the most useful information. We managed to totally can our latest project and built a new one by the time we hit the airport to head home!

> Thank you for your excellent presentation at the conference today. In a sentence, it was very inspiring.

> Your session was unreal. Very engaging, honest and fun.

> Your presentation was simply fantastic! A lesson in how to take the dull and boring and make it fun and entertaining.

Made in United States
Orlando, FL
04 November 2026

90202233R00070